SIMPLICITY: ESSAYS
JOSHUA FIELDS MILLBURN
& RYAN NICODEMUS

Asymmetrical Press
Columbia, Missouri
www.Asymmetrical.co

Published by Asymmetrical Press.

Library of Congress Cataloging-in-Publication Data
Simplicity: Essays / Millburn, Nicodemus — 4th ed.
Print ISBN: 978-1-938793-04-2
eISBN: 978-1-938793-05-9
WC: 23,178
1. Title. 2. Happiness. 3. Minimalism. 4. Simplicity. 5. Self-improvement.

Cover photo by Adam Dressler
Cover design by Dave LaTulippe

Author info:
Essays: theminimalists.com
Fiction: joshuafieldsmillburn.com
Email: themins@themins.com
Twitter: @JFM & @Ryan_Nicodemus

ASYM METR ICAL

Dedicated to our lovely readers. We appreciate you.

Simplicity is the ultimate sophistication.

—Leonardo da Vinci

simplicity: essays

PART ONE

INTRODUCTION

Foreword

About The Minimalists

Every journey has a direction *and* a destination. We started *The Minimalists* in December 2010 with two objectives in mind: to document our journey into minimalism and to inspire others to take a similar excursion if they found value in our message. We did not, however, expect the rapid growth we soon experienced. We knew our direction, but the eventual destination was a pleasant surprise.

It turns out that our message of *living a meaningful life with less stuff* resonated with a lot of people, people who were willing to share our message with their friends and family and coworkers. In less than a year, we were fortunate enough to witness the start of a small movement as our online audience grew to more than 100,000 monthly readers and we were featured in dozens of television, radio, print, and online media outlets, including the *Wall Street Journal*, NPR, CBC, CBS, FOX, and NBC. Moreover, our essays were featured on scores of popular websites, including *Zen Habits*, *Time* Magazine's #1 blog in the world.

But before we discovered minimalism, our lives were very different. Throughout much of our self-indulgent twenties, we "had it made." We were well-respected young professionals living the American Dream. Happiness was within our grasps. Or so we thought.

You see, back then we were two best friends, nearing age 30, living in Dayton, Ohio, with great six-figure jobs, luxury cars, big houses, plenty of toys, and an abundance of stuff. We had worked our way up the corporate ladder, gaining extensive experience leading large groups of people —hiring, coaching, and developing hundreds of employees.

But even with everything we had "accomplished," we were not satisfied with our lives. We were not content or fulfilled. We were not *truly* happy. And we discovered that working 70–80 hours a week and buying even more stuff didn't fill the void. In fact, it did the opposite: instead of happiness, our excessive accumulation of material possessions brought us debt and anxiety and stress and discontent and eventually a debilitating depression. As our lives spiraled out of control, we realized that we'd lost sight of everything that was truly important.

So in 2010, using the principles of minimalism, we took back control of our lives, discovering a lasting contentment for which we had yearned for many years. We simplified everything, jettisoning a good percentage of our material possessions, paying off immense debt, downsizing where applicable, choosing to live more deliberately. Our website, www.theminimalists.com, documents in great detail our journey into minimalism and our continued growth through experimentation. Our first full-length nonfiction book, *Minimalism: Live a Meaningful Life*, chronicles our troubled pasts, our accidental discovery of minimalism, and the entire new world of happiness, contentment, and purpose we experienced after incorporating minimalism into our daily lives.

In 2011, we left our corporate jobs to focus full-time on our passions. Since then we have published two books about minimalism, written hundreds of essays about simple living, and embarked on a 33-city whirlwind tour across the United States and Canada, meeting many of our incredible readers, exchanging ideas and listening to their heartfelt stories of radical change. Both books went on to become bestsellers, allowing us to get our message into the hands and minds of people in 151 countries around the world.

About This Book

This book is a "best of" collection, containing forty-six of our most important essays—some short, some long—from 2011 and 2012. These essays are purposefully organized into three broad themes—*material possessions, intentional living,* and *personal relationships*—covering a variety of topics, viewpoints, and arguments within those themes.

The order herein is deliberate; this collection is meant to be read in sequence from beginning to end. Doing so will result in an experience that is different from reading the essays individually throughout the web, connecting various concepts that might otherwise seem unconnected. These essays were written to encourage you to think critically about the excess in your life and, ultimately, to take action towards living more intentionally.

As a special thank you to our readers, we also

included two never-before published essays in this collection: "Simplicity" and "The Worst Christmas Ever."

Whether you obtained this book from your local library, ordered it online, or a friend gave you a copy, we hope you enjoy it. If you do, we'd appreciate your help in spreading the message: please share this book with a friend, sign up for free essays on our website, and leave a helpful review on Amazon if you have a moment. We sincerely hope this book adds value to your life.

Joshua & Ryan

PART TWO

MATERIAL POSSESSIONS

What Is Minimalism?

So what is this whole *minimalism* thing all about? To tell you the truth, it's quite simple: to be a minimalist you must live with less than 100 things, and you can't own a car or a home or a television, and you can't have a career, and you have to be able to live in exotic hard-to-pronounce places all over the world, and you have to start a blog, and you can't have any children, and you have to be a young white male from a privileged background.

OK, we're joking. Obviously. But people who dismiss minimalism as some sort of fad usually mention any of the above "restrictions" as to why they could "never be a minimalist." The truth is that minimalism isn't about any of those things, but it can help you accomplish many of them if you'd like. If you desire to live with fewer material possessions or to not own a car or a television or to travel all over the world, then minimalism can lend a hand. But that's not the point.

Minimalism is a tool that can assist you in finding freedom. Freedom from fear. Freedom from worry. Freedom from overwhelm. Freedom from guilt. Freedom from depression. Freedom from the consumer culture we've built our lives around. Real freedom.

That doesn't mean there's anything inherently wrong with owning material possessions. Today's problem seems to be the meaning we assign to our stuff. We tend to give too much meaning to our things, often forsaking our health, our relationships, our passions, our personal growth, and our desire to contribute beyond ourselves. Want to own a car or a house? Great, have at it! Want to raise a family and have a career? If these things are important to you, then that's wonderful. Minimalism simply allows you to make these decisions more consciously, more deliberately.

There are plenty of successful minimalists who lead appreciably different lives. Our friend Leo Babauta has a family and six children and lives in San Francisco. Joshua Becker has a career he enjoys, a family he loves, and a house and a car in suburbia. Conversely, Colin Wright owns 51 things and travels all over the world, while Tammy Strobel and her husband live in a "tiny house" and are completely car-free in Portland. Even though each of these people is different, they all have two things in common: they are minimalists, and minimalism has allowed them to pursue purpose-driven lives.

But how can these people be so different and yet still be minimalists? That brings us back to our original question: *what is minimalism?* If we had to sum it up in a single sentence, we would say, *Minimalism is a tool used to rid yourself of life's excess in favor of focusing on what's important so you can find happiness, fulfillment, and freedom.*

Minimalism has helped us to:
- Eliminate our discontent
- Reclaim our time
- Live in the moment
- Pursue our passions
- Discover our missions
- Experience real freedom
- Create more, consume less
- Focus on our health
- Eliminate depression
- Grow as individuals
- Contribute beyond ourselves
- Rid ourselves of excess stuff
- Focus on what's important
- Discover purpose in our lives

By incorporating minimalism into our lives, we're finally able to find lasting happiness. And let's face it: that's what we're all looking for, isn't it? We all want to be happy. Minimalists search for happiness not through things, but through life itself. Thus, it's up to you to determine what is necessary and what is superfluous in *your* life.

Through our essays we intend to present to you ideas for how to achieve a minimalist lifestyle without adhering to a strict code or an arbitrary set of rules. A word of warning, though: It isn't easy to take the first steps, but your journey towards minimalism gets much easier—and more rewarding—the farther you go. The first steps often take radical changes in your mindset, actions, and habits. Fret not, we want to help. That's why we've documented our experiences, so you can learn from our failures and successes, applying what we've learned to your own situation, assisting you in leading a more meaningful life.

Simplicity
An Unpublished Essay

> *"Most of the luxuries, and many of the so-called comforts of life, are not only not indispensable, but positive hindrances to the elevation of mankind."*
>
> —Henry David Thoreau, *Walden*

Life is not always easy, but it can be simple. Quite simple, actually.

If we were to time travel back to the days when Thoreau lived in his small cabin at Walden Pond, we'd realize that man needs very little to live: food and shelter and (perhaps) clothing. Conveniently, the earth provides everything we need. Man has invented the need for everything else.

Items that were once an unthinkable extravagance for most—cars, homes, furniture, to name a few—have transformed into necessities for much of the Western world. Other items that rank next to necessities—books, lamp light, utensils, TVs, radios, etc.—are taken for granted these days, assumed not to be just necessities but *fixtures* of everyday life.

It's not our intention to argue that material

possessions are wrong or ill-natured. Rather, we'd like to posit that the problem defies summary and is much more difficult to analyze. Ultimately, the problem lies within us, within the significance we give to our things. Most people work thousands of hours a year to buy things they think they need, not questioning if they need those things at all. If we simply stopped to question our continuous consumption, we'd find that most of the stuff we think we need isn't even close to necessary. In fact, life would be much simpler, and perhaps even easier and certainly more rewarding, without many of the possessions we think we need.

Even though he wouldn't have called it *minimalism*, Thoreau was perhaps the first-known modern-day minimalist. He lived with very little, especially while writing *Walden*, relying on little more than the land for everything he needed, and he lived a fulfilled, transcendent life.

And yet today we act as if we need so much more than we actually need. We don't only act this way, we *feel* this way. Emotionally, we yearn for material possessions, captivated by advertisements, vacuumed by the trappings of consumer culture, looking to fill a void that *we* created. But all we must do to break the cycle is pause, step back and think about our actions, our purchases, our true needs. Stuff will never fill the void, only a meaningful life will.

This life is short, but it contains everything. There is an inherent beauty in simplicity. Choose your path wisely; often the simple route is the most beautiful path to follow.

Questioning Stuff

Have you ever looked around your home and wondered why you have so much stuff? Or do you, like most people, simply accept the stuff that's there because it's *your* stuff?

Instead of questioning why you have the stuff, do you just spend hours organizing it, cleaning it, and occasionally replacing it if it "needs" to be replaced?

We did that too. For many, many years. And like us, you too can break the cycle.

Look around. Pick up something you haven't used in a while. Hold it in your hands. Feel it. Look it over. Think about it. When was the last time you really *needed* this thing? If you haven't used it in a while, why do you still have it? Are you holding on to it *just in case*?

Questioning the meaning we give to our stuff is the basis of minimalism. By paring down and getting rid of life's excess, we can focus on what's important.

There isn't anything wrong with owning stuff. The problem occurs when we give too much meaning to the stuff we own without questioning why we own it.

Over the last couple years, the two of us have questioned everything, from our clothes and our furniture, to our homes and our cars.

Question something today. Question something tomorrow. Discover a meaningful life. Lather, rinse, repeat.

The Consumption Continuum

Consumption is a continuum that covers an expansive range, with monk-like ascetics on one end and ready-for-reality-TV hoarders on the other.

But consumption alone isn't an inherently bad or evil thing. Actually, it isn't a *thing* at all—it's an action.

While minimalists are closer to the ascetics than the hoarders on this continuum, minimalism itself is far more concerned with living intentionally, living elegantly through simplicity, living purposefully while enjoying the material possessions you own without giving those possessions too much significance.

Thus, the problem isn't *consumption*; the problem is *we the people. We* are the problem. When we give too much meaning to the stuff we buy, when we think it will bring us happiness or contentment, we are setting ourselves up for failure.

Happiness doesn't work that way. Contentment is internal, and it is possible to be content with nothing *or* with a room full of stuff.

We'd suggest to you, however, that it's much easier to see what's important when you get the excess stuff out of the way, when you clear your path, opening your heart and your mind to the possibilities ahead. A sunset is more beautiful when you remove the blinders.

UnAmerican Dream

The American Dream...

The white picket fence. The large suburban home. The nice car. The big-screen TVs glowing in multiple rooms. The safe, reasonable nine-to-five. The corner office. The suit and tie. The white-collar pride. The blue-collar pride. The after-work gatherings. The weekends off. The paid holidays. The occasional vacation. The corporate credit card. The 401k account. The pension plan. The fringe benefits.

In exchange for...

The daily grind. The nose to the grindstone. The rush-hour traffic. The punching the clock. The cubical farms. The spreadsheet eyestrain. The much-anticipated lunch break. The inbox overflow. The arbitrary goals. The late nights at the office. The empty platitudes. The office gossip. The "productivity." The downsizing. The "doing more with less." The mounds of bills. The second job. The credit-card spending. The debt. The second mortgage. The beer gut. The mid-life crisis. The retirement at 65. The volatile stock market. The retirement delayed to 67 or 72 or 75. The death before retirement. The unyielding tiredness. The emptiness. The depression. The unshakeable discontent.

You can keep your American Dream. Give us back our time, our freedom, and our lives.

Getting Rid of Just In Case: 20/20 Theory

People often hold on to things *just in case* they need them. It's hard for us to let go because we *might* need something in the future. We pack too much stuff for trips and vacations *just in case* we might need it.

But we needn't hold on to these things *just in case*. The truth is, we rarely use these *just in case* items. Thus, they sit there, take up space, get in the way, weigh us down. Most of the time they aren't items we need at all.

Instead, if we remove the *just in case* items from our lives, we can get them out of the way, we can free up the space they consume.

Over the last year, the two of us let go of nearly all our *just in case* items. And during our 33-city meetup tour, we made sure we didn't pack any *just in case* items. None.

And then we tested our theory...

20/20 Theory

Anything we get rid of that we need later, we can replace for less than $20 and in less than 20 minutes from our current location. Thus far, this theory has held true 100% of the time. Although we've rarely had to replace a *just in case* item (less than five times this year for the two of us combined), we've never had to pay more than $20 or go more than 20 minutes out of our way to replace the item. This theory likely works 99% of the time for 99% of all items and 99% of all people. Including you.

More important, we haven't missed the hundreds of *just in case* items we got rid of, and we didn't need to replace most of them at all.

Getting rid of these items clears your mind, frees up your space and takes the weight off of your shoulders.

What are you holding on to *just in case*?

How Do I Get Him to Stop Watching the Damn TV?

A reader recently wrote seeking our advice:

I am working on creating a minimalist lifestyle for my family, but I have hit a roadblock and hope you can help, especially from the male perspective. In our house we watch TV, always have. I despise the TV because my husband spends so much time watching sports, it's often used as a babysitter for our kids when I am not home, it costs us money (granted the cable doesn't cost that much), and most of all it sucks up our time!

What, if any, suggestions do you have to get this time-sucker out of my house without causing a war with my husband? He is embracing minimalism, at least in theory, because while we didn't have tons of stuff, we got rid of lots of junk and he likes the feeling of more space, but I mention his beloved TV and it's a whole different ballgame.

Our recommendations:

Start with yourself. Before you can convince anyone to change, you must first change yourself.

Reduce. How many TVs do you have? If it's more than one, reduce the number by half at first. Get down to one TV over time.

Bedroom. Whatever you do, get the TV out of the bedroom. There are other ways to entertain each other in the bedroom without a TV.

Schedule. Schedule your viewing. Don't watch television unless you have scheduled your viewing at least 24 hours in advance. Ask your husband to test this with you for 10 days (an experiment of sorts).

Limit. Limit yourself to X hours per week. Track your viewing. Do this together for 10 days.

Friends. Invite friends over to watch TV with you (your scheduled viewing). Then talk about what you watched afterwards. This can strengthen your relationships.

Replace. Replace TV with other activities. Just getting rid of TV is boring—what else can you do together instead of watch television?

Once you do these things, your husband will likely follow. There's nothing wrong with owning a TV (Ryan has one, but no cable); it's when we spend too much time watching television that it has a negative effect on our lives.

Letting Go of Your DVD Collection

Are you one of those people who collects DVDs, proudly displaying your stockpile on a wall or shelf or special area designated for your dozens of favorite movies?

Have you ever thought about why you own all those DVDs? Do you plan to re-watch the same movies three or four times? If so, could you spend your time more wisely?

Both of us had fairly sizable DVD collections before taking our journeys into minimalism. We wasted thousands of dollars on these collections, often purchasing movies we'd already seen. And then we allowed our extensive collections to collect dust. Or we'd occasionally re-watch a movie, living in the past, attempting to reconstruct an old moment instead of creating new ones.

But *collecting* is just *hoarding* with a prettier name. Don't believe us? Look it up. *The Oxford American Writer's Thesaurus* lists the following synonyms under the first definition of *collection*: HOARD, pile, heap, stockpile.

Yes, collecting things you don't need—things from which you don't get value—is tantamount to hoarding. Even worse, watching the same movie over and over and over is, by definition, insane.

Sure, the two of us still watch movies, but we watch

new movies, creating new experiences in our lives; we strengthen our relationships by enjoying movies with friends; we grow by talking about those experiences after they happen, developing a better understanding of ourselves in the process.

So let go of that DVD collection (you can sell it and make some money), and stop watching the same things over and over. Instead, live your life. There is an entire world out there. And there is so much value you can add to that world, so much you can contribute beyond yourself—we're certain of it.

Don't Upgrade

The newest, latest, greatest version of Product X is available today. It's *only* X dollars and it does all the cool things you never knew it could do. And if you act now, Product X will change your life.

But we know we don't need Product X to live a meaningful life (even if we really, really want it). We know we don't have to buy the new iPhone when our old phone works just fine. We know we don't need a new car just because the old one isn't as shiny. And we know we don't need the latest version of software or iPad or television or laptop or gadget to make us happy.

Advertisers spend millions of dollars to create a sense of urgency to make us drool over their products. But we can refuse to play that game. We can turn down the noise. We can focus on *what we have* instead of what we don't have. After all, we already have everything we need.

Sure, sometimes things break or wear out over time. And when things break we are left with at least three options:

Go without. This option is almost taboo in our culture. It seems radical to many people. *Why would I go without when*

I could just buy a new one? But often this option is the best option. When we go without, it forces us to question our stuff, it forces us to discover whether we need it. And sometimes we discover that life without it is actually better than before.

Repair it. Sometimes we can't necessarily go without. Instead of running out and procuring Product X, we can attempt to repair the item first. You wouldn't buy a new car just because the brakes needed to be replaced, would you? The same goes for many other household items.

Replace it. As a last resort, we can replace things. Even when we do this, we can do so mindfully. We can purchase used items, we can buy products from local businesses, and often we can downgrade and still have what's necessary.

Getting Rid of Gifts

Our culture is a gift-giving culture, one that places great emphasis on giving physical items to other people as a measurement of caring. It seems silly to even write that, but it's the cold truth. We often give gifts to show that we care.

So, on your birthday and a handful of holidays, people acknowledge that they care about you. But don't they care about you those other 350+ days every year? Or do they feel different about you those days because they aren't giving you a physical item? (A new possession that you likely don't want anyway.)

Minimalist Gift Giving

We tend to not give gifts to people. Not physical gifts anyway.

We would much rather give an experience to someone than another material item. We'd rather give a loved one concert tickets than a necktie or an oven mitt.

We don't buy gifts; we give experiences, which leads to stronger relationships, greater growth and contribution, and ultimately a more fulfilling life.

A few experiences we love to gift:
- Concert or movie tickets
- A great home-cooked meal
- A meal at a nice restaurant
- Walking somewhere without a plan
- Write something nice about someone publicly
- A personal massage
- Our attention
- Our time

These are things we can do *with* other people, experiences that show we care.

When to Give Gifts

The worst time to give a gift is on someone's birthday or a holiday. Think about it. There is already an expectation to give gifts at these times, and it's a hard expectation to live up to.

The best time to give a gift is today, right now, for absolutely no reason at at all. The best real reason to give an experiential gift is to say, "I care about you" or "I love you" or "You are important to me" or "Thank you for being in my life." Our actions need to be congruent with our feelings, and giving a gift today shows that every day is a special occasion, it shows the people in your life that they are just as important as they are on any holiday.

Minimalist Gift Getting

The two of us tend to not accept physical gifts from other people. Sometimes it's hard to get other people to understand this cultural shift. The best way to approach the no-gift-getting concept is to be proactive. We set the expectation with our friends and family that we don't need any more stuff, and if they want to give us gifts, they can get us experiences we will enjoy, they can celebrate our lives with us by spending time with us, not by giving us stuff.

What does a minimalist do about gifts they already own?

Most of us don't want to piss people off. We don't want to offend other people. We worry what they will think about us.

We recently received an interesting comment/question from a reader:

I recently started my minimalist journey, and up until now everything I have let go of has been pretty easy. However, I am having trouble getting rid of gifts. It's not me who has a problem getting rid of them, it's the people who gave them to me who might get a bit upset. I was wondering if you had any suggestions? I want to get rid of this stuff because I feel like it is holding me up from moving on with my new lifestyle but I do not want to offend anyone.

Our Response

Most people won't notice or won't care.

But a few people might get offended. And that's OK.

When we left our corporate jobs, some people got offended. When we stopped checking email every day, some people got offended. When we said "no" to certain past commitments, some people got offended. When we stopped buying certain material possessions, some people got offended. When we untethered from negative relationships, some people got offended.

We can't let these things bother us though.

So get rid of the stuff if it's not adding value to your life—donate it, sell it, or trash it. Let go of it so you can focus on what's important. Most people won't even notice when you get rid of your old gifts. If they do, explain to them that you're paring down your material possessions so you can be happier. After all, the reason they got you the gift in the first place was because they thought it would make you happy.

The Blackest of Fridays

> *Black (adj.): characterized by tragic*
> *or disastrous events; causing despair.*
> —New Oxford American Dictionary

In the United States, the day after Thanksgiving is the busiest shopping day of the year: Black Friday. Retailers prepare months in advance for this day—preparation that's meant to stimulate your insatiable desire to consume.

Doorbuster sales. New products. Gigantic newspaper ads. TV, radio, print, billboards. Sale, sale, sale! Early bird specials. One day only! Get the best deal. Act now! While supplies last.

Consumption is an unquenchable thirst. Both of us understand this too well. In our corporate careers of yesteryear, we both managed large numbers of retail stores.

The pernicious aspects of Black Friday are not few. The pandemonium of this day is a metaphor of our consumer culture. On this day, people consume gluttonously without regard for the harm they're inflicting on themselves. On this day, greed becomes ravenous. On this day, people live without real meaning, buying gifts to fill a void that can't possibly be filled with any amount of material possessions.

But there are better ways to live life.

Sadly, people participate in the rapacious nature of Black Friday in the name of a holiday—as if buying gifts was an ideal way to celebrate Christmas.

We can, however, make this year different. We can refuse to buy material items for people to display our love. We can showcase our love, caring, and affection through our daily actions—every day, not just holidays.

If still you want to give a gift to someone, why not gift an experience—like a nice meal, tickets to a concert or play, or a sunset on the beach? After all, the best, most loving gift you can give someone is your time and undivided attention.

Will you join us? Will you opt out of Black Friday? If not, why not?

The Worst Christmas Ever
An Unpublished Essay

> *"How come everything I think I need always comes with*
> *batteries? What do you think it means?"*
> —John Mayer, "Something's Missing"

Little Andrew unwrapped Optimus Prime on Christmas morning and a smile broke across his features as the large toy lit up and nearly came to life, flashing and beeping and driving Andy's parents crazy.

But in a few moments, Andy discarded the toy and began unwrapping the rest of his presents, extracting each box from under the tree, one by one—some long, some tall, some heavy, some light. Each shiny, painstakingly-wrapped box revealed a new toy. Each shred of green-and-red wrapping paper, a flash of happiness.

An hour later, however, little Andy was crying hysterically, throwing a tantrum while staring at the empty spaces between his new toys. Based on his fits, this had undoubtedly been the worst Christmas ever.

Sure, Andrew had received many of the things on his list, but he was far more concerned with what he hadn't

JOSHUA FIELDS MILLBURN & RYAN NICODEMUS

received. The toys in front of him simply reminded him of what he didn't have.

Don't we, as adults, do the same thing? Don't we often look at the things around us and wish we had more? Don't we covet that brand new car, those trendy new clothes, that expensive new gadget?

What if little Andy was happy with the toys in front of him?

What if we were, too?

10/10 Material Posessions Theory

How important is the *stuff* in your life?

Your material possessions—those things you've worked so hard for, slaving 40, 50, 60 hours a week to acquire—how much value do they actually add to your day-to-day life?

We bet it's less than you realize.

Here's an exercise for you. Take a moment, write down your **10 most expensive material possessions from the last decade**. Things like your car, your house, your jewelry, your furniture, and any other material possessions you own or have owned in the last ten years. The big ticket items.

Next to that list, make another top 10 list: **10 things that add the most value to your life**. This list might include experiences like catching a sunset with a loved one, watching your kid play baseball, eating dinner with your parents, etc.

Be honest with yourself when you're making these lists. It's likely that the lists share *zero* things in common.

What if, instead of focusing the majority of your time, attention, and energy on the 10 most expensive material possessions, you shifted your focus towards the 10 things that added the most value to your life? How would that make you feel? How would your life be different a month from now? A year from now? Five years from now?

Essay inspired by Geoffrey Miller's book, Spent.

More Is Less?

Less is more. We all know the saying. It has been transformed into a platitude by advertisers and TV shows and even corporate America as it right-sizes people out of their livelihoods ("We'll have to learn to do more with less around here."). But is less *really* more? And if so, is the opposite true? Is more actually less?

Questions like this may be more important than you think.

The two of us enjoy taking commonly accepted truisms and trite stock phrases and flipping them on their axes, exploring the other sides of clichés and hackneyed phrases, shedding light on the opposite sides of supposed facts.

For example, what moniker does our culture often assign to a well-adjusted, ostensibly successful person? We often say these people are *anchored* (i.e., "He is such an anchored person."). We used to hear this term frequently during our late twenties. We were regularly described as anchored people. And for the longest time we took this as a compliment.

But then we stopped taking it at face value and asked, "What is an anchor?"

That question led us to an important discovery about our own lives: an anchor is the thing that keeps a ship at bay, planted in the harbor, stuck in one place, unable to explore the freedom of the sea. Perhaps we were anchored—we knew we weren't happy with our lives—and perhaps being anchored wasn't necessarily a good thing.

In the course of time, we each identified our own personal anchors—circumstances keeping us from realizing real freedom—and found they were plentiful (Joshua catalogued 83 anchors; Ryan, 54). We discovered big anchors (debt, bad relationships, etc.) and small anchors (superfluous bills, material possessions, etc.) and in time we eliminated the vast majority of those anchors, one by one, documenting our experience in our book, *Minimalism: Live a Meaningful Life*.

It turned out that being anchored was a terrible thing; it kept us from leading the lives we wanted to lead. No, not all our anchors were bad, but the vast majority prevented us from encountering lasting contentment.

Are you an anchored person? Is that a good thing? What are some of your anchors? And what other axioms might you want to question?

Which brings us back to our original set of questions: Is less really more? If so, is more actually less?

We'd suggest the answer to both is *yes*.

Owning less stuff, focusing on fewer tasks, and having less in the way, has given us more time, more freedom, and more meaning in our lives. Working less allows us to contribute more, grow more, and pursue our passions much more than before.

Similarly, having more time causes less frustration and less stress, more freedom adds less anxiety and less worry, and more meaning in our lives allows us to focus far less on life's excess in favor of what's truly important.

So, more is less? Yes, more or less.

Decluttering Doesn't Work Like That

Decluttering is, by and large, a farce. If you went to our website or picked up one of our books just to figure out how to declutter your closet, then you went to the wrong place. You'll be hard pressed to find anything here even vaguely resembling something as trite as *67 Ways to Declutter a Messy Home*. That's because decluttering alone doesn't solve the problem; discussing how to get rid of your stuff answers only the *what*, but not the *why*.

The *what*—i.e., the *how to*—is easy. We all know, instinctively, *how to* declutter. You can start small: focus on one room at a time, making progress each day as you work towards a simplified life. You can go big: rent a dumpster and throw out everything, moving on to a more meaningful life. Or you can take the moderate approach: plunge into a Packing Party and embrace the fun side of decluttering, enjoying the entire simplification process (for details on our packing party, visit www.theminimalists.com/day3).

People should, however, be much more concerned with the *why*—the *purpose* behind decluttering—than the *what*. While the *what* is easy, the *why* is far more abstruse and difficult to discuss, because the nature of the *why* is highly individual. Ultimately, the *why* has to do with the benefits *you'll* experience once you're on the other side of decluttering.

Decluttering is not the end result; it is merely the first step. You don't become instantly happy and content by just getting rid of all your stuff—at least not in the long run. Decluttering doesn't work like that. You see, if you simply embrace the *what* without the *why*, then you'll get nowhere (slowly and painfully, by the way, repeatedly making the same mistakes). It is possible to get rid of everything you own and still be utterly miserable, to come home to your empty house and sulk after removing all your pacifiers.

When you get rid of the vast majority of your possessions you're forced to confront your darker side: *Why did I give so much meaning to material possessions? What is truly important in life? Why am I discontent? Whom is the person I want to become? How will I define my own success?*

These are difficult questions without easy answers. But these questions are far more important than just jettisoning your material possessions. If you don't answer them carefully, rigorously, then the closet you just decluttered will be brimming with new purchases not long from now.

Organizing Is Nothing But Well-Planned Hoarding

We need to start thinking of *organizing* as a dirty word. It is, in fact, a sneaky little profanity—a pernicious little booger—that keeps us from simplifying our lives.

Our televisions would have us believe that there's a battle being fought on the consumption continuum, a battle between the organizers and the hoarders. And from our couches it's hard to see who's winning.

We'd assert, however, that these two sides are working together, colluding to achieve the same thing: the accumulation of more stuff. One side—the hoarders—does so overtly, leaving everything out in the open, making them easy targets to sneer at. But the other side—the sneaky organizers—are more covert, more systematic, more devious when it comes to the accumulation of stuff. Ultimately, though, organizing is nothing more than well-planned hoarding.

Sure, both sides go about their hoarding differently, but the end result is not appreciably different. Whether our homes are strewn with wall-to-wall material possessions or we have a complex ordinal item-dispersal system, color-coded and alphabetized, we're still not dealing with the real problem.

No matter how organized we are, we must continue to care for the stuff we organize, cleaning and sorting our methodically structured belongings. When we get rid of the superfluous stuff, however, we can focus on life's more important aspects. Said another way: We can spend the day focusing on our health, on our relationships, on pursuing what we're passionate about. Or we could, of course, reorganize our basement again.

Consumerism

I'm the pack of lies that keeps you "safe."

I'm the thoughts you're too ashamed to share.

I'm the crushing feeling you feel inside.

I'm the memory you can't get out of your head.

I'm the lust, the empty desire.

I'm the fear, the greed.

I'm the Black Friday, the Cyber Monday.

I'm the impulse, the hurry-up-and-buy, the just-one-more.

I'm the cocaine-high that doesn't last past the checkout line.

I'm the sound of money washing down the drain.

I am consumerism.

Give me a chance.

I promise you won't be satisfied.

Essay inspired by David Gray's "Nemesis"

The Compelling Beauty of Free

Life can be mighty expensive inside the flashy walls of our consumer culture. Dinner and a movie. Daily venti lattes. That cute new outfit. Those cute new shoes to go with that cute new outfit. The price of a couple hotdogs and a beer at a ball game. Not to mention all your bills. Gas. Electric. Mortgage. Car payments. Insurance. Credit cards. Student loans. Add it all up and it can be crippling financially. It's terrifying to even think about.

But not everything costs an arm and a leg. *The best things in life are free* is an overused platitude; but the nice thing about platitudes is they're often true—they are often maxims by which we could improve our lives if we didn't dismiss them as overly trite or vapid.

Thus, the best things in life are, in fact, free. Love. Relationships. Health. Personal growth. Contribution. Six-pack abs.

But we'd like to suggest to you that nearly everything you need to enjoy your life is free as well. Sure you need money to pay for certain necessities, but most aspects of your life have the potential to cost you nothing; the system is already set up to make your most enjoyable experiences free.

Exercise is free when you do it at home or in the park

or anywhere that doesn't cost a fee. **Walking** through your city and taking in the beauty of it all is free. Listening to **music** you already love is free. A glass of tap **water** is free. While your food costs money, choosing **healthy food** over junk food is free. **Reading** a book is free. **Writing** about your life—or someone else's life—is free. Wearing your favorite **clothes**—your favorite teeshirt, jeans, and shoes—is free.

Lovemaking is free. Sitting with a friend or a lover under the stars and **laughing** together is free. Going to a friend's house and **watching a movie** together is free. **Donating** your time to help out at a local soup kitchen is free. **Sitting** in a quiet room and enjoying your time alone is free. The air you **breathe** is free.

Most important, your **freedom** is free, though we often spend a lot of time and money just to give it up.

PART THREE

INTENTIONAL LIVING

The Definition of Success

"Success without happiness is failure."
—Anthony Robbins

A Simple Equation

For us, success is a simple equation:

Happiness + Constant Improvement + Contribution =
Success

That's the only kind of success we know. If we're not happy, then we're not successful.

We weren't successful when we had corporate careers and the fancy things that our culture told us made us successful. We weren't successful because we weren't satisfied with that life; we weren't happy or fulfilled or content.

Thus, success consists of three things: being happy with who you are and what you're doing, constantly growing as an individual, and contributing to other people in meaningful ways. If these three things are present, then you're successful.

Successfool

We used to be "successful." At least that's what everyone said.

People frequently told us that we had things "figured out," because by age 27 we both worked "great" six-figure jobs, we were climbing the corporate ladder, and we owned all the things that were supposed to make us happy: the big houses, the luxury cars, the fancy material possessions.

But we sure didn't feel like we had it figured out. And we certainly didn't feel successful either. Instead, we felt overwhelmed by the so-called success in our lives. We were unhealthy, unfulfilled, and our lives lacked purpose. The long hours we worked and the stuff we bought didn't fill the void we felt inside.

Unfortunately, we'd subscribed to the ridiculous cultural standards promulgated by our heavily mediated society. Despite what people said, we *weren't* successful. Rather, we were fools: successfools.

You needn't be fooled like we were by the false cultural pressures propagated by the ads on TV, proliferated by the ghosts haunting the cubical farms at your job.

A six-figure job doesn't make you successful. There's nothing wrong with earning money, but the money alone will not make you happy.

A shiny new car doesn't make you successful. There's nothing wrong with owning things you enjoy, but your material possessions alone will not bring you bliss.

Consider your daily actions. Do you pacify yourself with short-term pleasures, sacrificing true success and happiness and fulfillment for ephemeral pellets of momentary gratification?

Are you truly successful? Are you happy? Do you feel fulfilled? Are you living a purpose-filled life? You can. And, more importantly, you deserve to.

Choose your daily actions wisely. Meaningless short-term pleasure often equals long-term suffering, while short-term pain can offer you long-term joy and growth and contentment. The choice is yours to make.

Grow Yourself, Not Your Stuff

Before we discovered minimalism and understood the importance of simplifying our lives, we were successful young professionals from Dayton, Ohio. But we were only ostensibly successful.

You see, back then, people saw two best friends in their large homes with more bedrooms than inhabitants and they were envious. They saw our six-figure jobs, our luxury cars, our new gadgets, and our lives of opulence, and they thought, "These guys know what they're doing. I want to be just like them." They saw all those things—all that superfluous stuff—and they just knew we were successful. After all, we were living the American Dream, weren't we?

But the truth is we weren't successful at all.

Maybe we looked successful—displaying our status symbols as if they were trophies—but we weren't truly successful. Because even with all our stuff, we weren't satisfied with our lives, we weren't happy. And we discovered that working 70 to 80 hours a week and buying even more stuff didn't fill the void. In fact, it only brought us more debt and anxiety and fear and loneliness and guilt and overwhelm and paranoia and depression. It was a solipsistic existence.

Even worse, we discovered that we didn't have control of our time and thus we didn't have control of our own lives.

And then, as our lives were spiraling downward in ever-diminishing circles toward empty oblivion, we inadvertently discovered minimalism. It was a beacon in the night. We lingered curiously on the limbic portions of its perimeter, scouring feverishly through internet page after internet page looking for more information and guidance and enlightenment, watching and learning and attempting to understand what this whole "simple living" thing was all about. Through months of research we traveled further and further down the rabbit hole, and over time we discovered a group of people without a lot of things but with myriad happiness and passion and freedom—things for which we yearned so desperately.

Eventually we embraced simple lives, we embraced minimalism as a way of life and discovered that we too could be happy, but it wasn't through owning more stuff, it wasn't through accumulation. We took back control of our lives so we could focus on what's important, so we could focus on life's deeper meaning, so we could focus on finding true and lasting happiness.

Happiness, as far as we're concerned, is achieved through living a meaningful life—a life that is filled with passion and freedom, a life in which we grow as individuals and contribute to other people in meaningful ways. Growth and contribution—those are the bedrocks of happiness. Not stuff. This may not sound sexy or marketable or sellable, but it's the cold truth. As humans, we're happy if we're growing as individuals and contributing beyond ourselves.

Without growth, and without a deliberate effort to help others, we are simply slaves to cultural expectations, ensnared by the trappings of money and power and status and perceived success.

Minimalism is a tool that allowed us to simplify our lives so we could focus on what's important. We were able to strip away the excess stuff and focus on living meaningful lives.

We invite you to join us. Membership is free. And you deserve to be happy. You deserve to live a meaningful life, too.

Everybody Worships Something
Conscious Freedom: Part One

"In the day-to-day trenches of adult life, there is actually no such thing as atheism. There is no such thing as not worshipping. Everybody worships. The only choice we get is what to worship. And the compelling reason for maybe choosing some sort of God or spiritual-type thing is that pretty much anything else you worship will eat you alive. If you worship money and things, if they are where you tap real meaning in life, then you will never feel you have enough. Worship your body and beauty and sexual allure and you will always feel ugly, and when time and age start showing, you will die a million deaths before they finally grieve you. Worship power, you will end up feeling weak and afraid, and you will need ever more power over others to numb you to your own fear. Worship your intellect, you will end up feeling like a fraud, always on the verge of being found out."

—David Foster Wallace, *This Is Water*

This is Not a Sermon

If you are worried that this is some sort of preachy, didactic sermon about why you should worship God or why you shouldn't or what you should worship at all, don't be.

Whatever you believe spiritually, we have nothing to offer you with respect to spiritual guidance.

Rather, this essay is about our unconscious obsession with things. And not just physical things, but our overwhelming obsession with all of life's misguided devotions. This essay is about how to deal with that unconscious obsession.

What's Important In Your Life?

What is important to you? Do you know? Have you made an *important-things* list for your life? If you did, it would probably include things like family, friends, relationships, personal health, contributing to others, personal growth, personal goals, spirituality, etc. These are the things that are most important to most people. But if we were to walk around your home, would we be able to tell what's important to you? Would the *things* in your home coincide with your *important-things* list?

If you are like we were before our journey into minimalism, then the answer is undoubtedly *no*. Not even close.

If you were to visit either of our homes back then, you would have thought our *important-things* list contained things like DVDs and neckties and consumer electronics and shoes and hall closets stuffed with coats and junk drawers brimming with junk.

Sure we had pictures of family members strewn throughout our places, and we even had some seldom-used exercise equipment that was supposed to aid us in our physical health. So, yes, the important things were there, but

71

they were hard to notice because they were hidden amongst the clutter, camouflaged by superfluous excess.

Material possessions are not immoral or evil, nor is our love for those things. The insidious thing about our love for stuff is that it's unconscious. We often worship the things in our life without knowing that we worship them at all. We place value and meaning in things, things that don't mean anything to us—not really. And over time this worship—this misplaced value—can be pernicious and ultimately self-destructive.

Say It Out Loud

One thing that helps us these days is to say something out loud. There is an unavoidable ridiculousness factor to incongruent statements when we say them out loud. Go on, give it a try. Let's start with the easy ones, the ones that *won't* sound ridiculous. Let's start with the important things in your life. Say these things out loud. Heck, shout them if you feel like it:

- My family is *incredibly important* to me.
- It is *immensely important* for me to contribute to other people in a meaningful way.
- I don't know where I would be without my close friends, they are *so important* to me.
- It is *extremely important* for me to live a healthy life.
- It is *important* for me to [blank].

Did you say them out loud? Really? See, none of those

things sound ridiculous. That's because they are congruent with your beliefs; they coincide with the tone, passion, and conviction of the statements themselves.

But try these on for size. Try to say these things out loud with the same conviction and passion and feel the difference. Come on, no one's looking:

- This T-shirt is *incredibly important* to me.

- It is *immensely important* for me to go to the mall and shop today.

- I don't know where I would be without my khaki pants, they are *so important* to me.

- It is *extremely important* for me to eat that extra piece of pie.

You get the point. Ridiculous, right? They are ridiculous even though they are the same sentences structurally. You just replaced a few words when you said them out loud.

Again, we don't think any of these things are wrong or evil. It's OK to wear khakis and to eat pie and to have material possessions. But of course we all know that none of these things are truly important either. We know that they have no real meaning in our lives. And yet we often act as if the stuff in our lives is just as important—or worse, more important—than the things that actually matter to us, like our relationships, our health, our freedom.

Intellect vs. Emotion

You know these things already, though. We aren't telling

you anything new. You know that your blue jeans are not more important than your family, that your car is not more important than your health, that your designer cosmetics are not more important than contributing to other people who need your help. You *know* these things.

The problem is that you know these things *intellectually* but not *emotionally*. In other words, you don't feel it in your gut. Instead your emotional connection is often with the *stuff* in your life. You feel this connection to material items deep down in your gut, and you don't even have to think about it intellectually. It's easy to do this, it's easy to feel connected to your possessions. You never have to worry if your things will love you back, you never have to worry about them dying or losing interest in you or leaving you for someone else. And it feels good because there are not immediate consequences for loving stuff, there's even a cheap sort of instant gratification in doing so.

The events of our lives have conditioned us to feel this way, and thus we are hardwired to feel an emotional connection to *stuff*. Unfortunately, this is our *default setting*. There are many reasons we have this kind of hardwired default setting, some of which are inherently cultural, some of which have to do with inimically slick marketing, some of which have to do with our own belief templates that we've been molding ever since we've had the ability to piece together a solitary thought.

The reasons are irrelevant though.

Adjusting Your Default Setting

What *is* relevant is that it's *not your fault*. Or at least it's not your fault that your default setting is one in which you have an emotional connection to *stuff*. Just like it's not your fault that you speak whatever native language you speak. Sure, you learned the language over time, and, sure, you *could* choose to never speak another word of your native tongue, but you were raised to speak that language, and thus you will always have a connection to it; it will always be your default language. Similarly, at this point in your life, your connection to stuff is your default connection, it's your default setting, but that doesn't mean that you should be ashamed of it, just aware of it.

And so it may not be your *fault*, but it is your *responsibility* to adjust your default setting to one with real meaning, to become "well adjusted," which—as Wallace suggests in his above quoted essay—is not a coincidental term.

People who are "well adjusted" have a belief template in which their intellectual beliefs coincide with their emotional beliefs. A vast majority of the time this kind of self-adjustment is not accidental. It is utterly intentional. Aligning our intellectual and emotional beliefs is a conscious choice, and it is not an easy choice. It is also not a choice we make one time and then our personal beliefs are aligned forever.

It's like exercising. We don't go to the gym one day, workout really hard for a few hours, and then expect to be in great shape for the rest of our lives. It doesn't work that way. Sometimes it's incredibly difficult. Sometimes we feel like we can't do it. And sometimes after a long hard day we just don't want to do it at all.

Similarly, sometimes it feels easier to let our emotions take control of our beliefs. It's easy to whip out our American Express cards and buy that $200 dress at the mall. It's easy to pacify our kids with a Happy Meal. It's easy to set on the back-burner what's important to us, to put it off until tomorrow. But if we do this too often, if we continue to put off everything until tomorrow, tomorrow never comes.

And your authors do it even now, even after embracing a lifestyle of simplicity and minimalism and freedom of choice, we still do it. We fall back to our default setting. The key is to catch ourselves when we fall, to be conscious of our decisions and make quick adjustments to avoid our default setting. The key is to live a conscious life, one that is full of real meaning and happiness and fulfillment and freedom.

We wish you the best in your life. It's not always easy, but you deserve to live a conscious life, a life focused on what's important. After all, you live only one life; it's best that you're awake for it.

I Am Not the Center of the Universe

Conscious Freedom: Part Two

"Everything in my own immediate experience supports my deep belief that I am the absolute center of the universe, the realest, most vivid and important person in existence. We rarely think about this sort of natural, basic self-centeredness because it's so socially repulsive. But it's pretty much the same for all of us. [It's] hardwired into our boards at birth. Think about it: there is no experience you have had that you are not the absolute center of. The world as you experience it is there in front of YOU or behind YOU, to the left or right of YOU, on YOUR TV or YOUR monitor. Other people's thoughts and feelings have to be communicated to you, but your own are so immediate, urgent, real."

—David Foster Wallace, *This Is Water*

A Different Perspective

It's incredibly difficult to think about the world from a perspective other than our own. We're always worried about what's going on in our lives. What does my schedule look like today? What if I lose my job during the next round of layoffs? Why can't I stop smoking? Why am I overweight? Why am I not happy with my life?

Suffice it to say that we are acutely aware of everything

connected to our own lives. Everything good, everything bad. Everything in our lives.

Of course we also worry about other people as well. But not with the same intensity, not with the same level of focus or connection, and not with the same ferocious subconscious vigor that we apply to our own lives. When we worry, it's fundamentally about ourselves and how the events going on around us impact us.

Contribution

This is true even for the so-called benevolent activities of our lives. Think about it. When we contribute to others, why do we do it?

I do it to help others, you might say.

That's probably true, but why do we want to help others?

Because it makes them feel better.

Also true, but why do we want them to feel better?

Because it makes me happy when I make other people happy.

Ah! Exactly. It makes *you* happy.

To be clear, there is nothing wrong with helping others. And there is nothing wrong with feeling good about helping others either. You *should* feel good about it. Your authors make an effort to help others all the time. We donate our time to local charities and non-profit organizations, and we make a conscious effort to contribute to people in a meaningful way. In fact, that's the reason why we created theminimalists.com, to help people. Contribution is an amazing virtue.

But this essay is not about virtues. We're not attempting to preach to you about being virtuous or give you reasons why you should donate your time to charitable organizations or convert you to a life of monk-like dedication to a righteous cause.

Rather, this essay is about consciously removing yourself from the center of the universe. It's about paying attention to what's going on in front of you and around you and inside you. That's a tall order, we know.

And Yet You Are Not the Center of the Universe

It's a tall order because it's not easy to control your thoughts, minute after minute, hour after hour, day after day. We'd like to posit to you that gaining control of your thoughts—of what's going on inside you—is the key to real happiness, it's the key to real freedom.

It might not sound fun or sexy or exciting, but it's the cold truth. If you can remove yourself—if you can remove your perspective—from a situation, then you can see the world through a different set of eyes, and thus the world can take on a different meaning.

What we are really talking about here is a certain ideology—an American and Western ideology—that says "I am the most important person on earth, and what I want is the most important thing and that my main job in life is to gratify my own desires."

It might sound crude or even repulsive to think this way, but it's true. This ideology is perpetrated by television and advertising and entertainment and a culture of endless consumption, so much so that our own economy thrives on it. It's the way life is, we are all in our own little bubbles, all more important than the people around us. And while this may not be universally true for every person in the culture, it is true for the culture as a whole; it's a fairly accurate way to summarize the ethos of our culture.

And of course nobody tells us this. Our parents didn't sit us down when we were little and tell us that this is the way it is, that we are the center of our own universe. Instead, it is subtle and gradual and is delivered by a great number of messages. Our culture is one enormous template of self-indulgence and self-gratification and self-advancement.

And yet in some ways this solipsistic template works very well. It has created massive amounts of wealth for many Westerners, it works great for short-term commerce (i.e., for selling us stuff we don't need), and it allows us to build our own individual-sized kingdoms, with our McMansions as palaces, our luxury cars as chariots, and our stuff as the humble servants of our kingdoms (at least ostensibly).

And in other ways—ways that are often much harder to discuss without sounding cliché or parable-ish or overly reductive—this template does not work well at all. There are parts of us that need to worry about things other than ourselves, things that are more important than us as individuals. The reasons these things are so hard to talk about is that they are usually not fun or exciting. It's easy to market the seductive pleasures of fast cars and big homes and expensive alcohol and excessive consumption—we do so masterfully with slick, concise, thirty-second flash-cut messages—but it is much harder to make selflessness and contribution and respect to others just as attractive, and it is nearly impossible to do so using the same mediums in a similarly attenuated timespan.

And yet, somewhat paradoxically, it's impossible to feel content without these things, it's impossible to feel fulfilled or satisfied if we do not contribute beyond ourselves.

The Rise of Minimalism

This is perhaps why the minimalist movement has grown legs as of late. Minimalism is a way to remove yourself from the center of it all, to remove yourself from the desire to chase excess in our pursuit of happiness.

Instead, minimalism shows us that there is happiness within us all already, that we are happy without unnecessary excess, without cars and boats and mansions and clothes and all the things of this world. Not that the things of this world are wrong or evil, it's just that they are not the point of our lives.

The point of our lives is much more complex, and yet minimalism can help make it more simple, more available, more real. That is the attractiveness of minimalism.

Minimalism is a tool that can help us regain our consciousness and show us that the real point of our lives is not consumption, and it's not to accumulate stuff. The real meaning of our lives is to contribute to other people in meaningful ways, to contribute beyond ourselves. It takes a special kind of awareness to break through our cultural imperatives to realize this, but when we do realize it, we can live a more meaningful life, one that is filled with passion and happiness and fulfillment and freedom.

Awareness: The Most Precious Kind of Freedom

Conscious Freedom: Part Three

"The so-called real world of men and money and power hums merrily along in a pool of fear and anger and frustration and craving and worship of self. Our own present culture has harnessed these forces in ways that have yielded extraordinary wealth and comfort and personal freedom. The freedom all to be lords of our tiny skull-sized kingdoms, alone at the center of all creation. This kind of freedom has much to recommend it. But of course there are all different kinds of freedom, and the kind that is most precious you will not hear talked about much in the great outside world of wanting and achieving. The really important kind of freedom involves attention and awareness."

—David Foster Wallace, 2005, *This Is Water*

Dave's Parable

David Foster Wallace begins the above quoted essay with a cute little story about two little fish who are swimming along and happen to meet an older fish swimming the other way. The older fish nods at them and says, "Morning, boys. How's the water?" The two young fish swim on for a bit, and then eventually one of them looks over at the other and says, "What the hell is water?"

Obviously, the point of Wallace's little parable is obvious: the things that should be the most obvious to us are often not that obvious at all. Confused yet? Well, in other words, we get so caught up and immersed in our day-to-day activities that we don't always notice what's going on around us. Or worse, we don't notice what's going on inside us— inside our heads, inside our hearts. In the case of the two young fish, they were unaware of their most obvious surroundings. They were unaware of the water that surrounded them, it was something that was everywhere, something that was so important and so essential for their survival, and yet they were unaware that it even existed.

What Is Your Water?

But how does this apply to our lives? Surely we're all bright enough to know which things are essential to our survival, right? And certainly we're all bright enough to know that we need air to breathe and food to eat, just like the fish needed water to live, right?

But perhaps our proverbial water is much deeper; perhaps it's much more complex. Although perhaps it's also just as obvious as the water should have been to the tiny little fish.

Maybe our water includes complex concepts like *happiness* and *fulfillment* and *freedom*. And while all these things are ostensibly abstract and abstruse, perhaps they are more obvious than we realize, and perhaps they are essential to us. Perhaps we need freedom like the fish needed water.

What is Freedom?

Freedom is a vast, complex concept, and it is difficult to define or explain or dissect. Freedom means different things to different people, and it takes on different meanings within different contexts. Perhaps that's why it took Jonathan Franzen nine years and nearly six hundred pages to explain *Freedom* in his novel with the same title.

What's even more complicated is that freedom is even harder to talk about as an event, and thus must be talked about as an abstraction, and that might be why Franzen had to write about it using stories and characters and a forty-year narrative, so that he could compare and contrast freedom with ideas like loneliness, love, desire, pain and solitude, none of which explain freedom, but perhaps together they begin to explain the essence of freedom.

A Certain Kind of Freedom

Like we said, it's very complicated. And that's why this essay is not about freedom as a general term (which could possibly take a circuitous 500-page college thesis that very few of you would want to read). Rather, this essay is about a certain kind of freedom: awareness. More specifically, it's about a certain kind of conscious acute awareness, an awareness of what's going on around you, an awareness of what's going on inside you. This kind of awareness—one in which you must constantly be attentive—is the most precious kind of freedom. It is, in many respects, the choice between life and death; it's the difference between living a meaningful life and being dead inside.

We realize that this kind of topic might sound like a lecture from a grandparent, and it's easy to dismiss it as a bunch of esoteric nonsense because it makes us feel better to not think about such things; it makes us feel better to live our day to day lives unaware. But this kind of unconscious living does not make us free; it makes us a slave to the world around us, reacting to our own impulses without thinking.

The Minimalist's Awareness

This is yet another reason why minimalism is so appealing to so many people. It removes many of the obstructions and allows us to focus on what's important. Minimalism is a tool to rid ourselves of superfluous excess in favor of a meaningful life. It is a tool to take a seemingly intricate and convoluted world, cluttered with its endless embellishments, and make it simpler, easier, realer.

It is unimaginably hard to remain conscious and attentive and aware. It is difficult not to fall back into a trance-like state, surrounded by the trappings and obstructions of the tiring world around us. But it is important to do so. It is important to remind yourself that this is your life, to remind yourself that your life is important, to remind yourself that you can make a difference, to remind yourself that you have a purpose on this earth, one that extends beyond yourself. It is important to remind yourself that *this is water*.

If, Then

"You're making up lies to justify your mood."
—Jay Nash, "Everything"

People concoct all kinds of excuses to explain their bad decisions:

If I had more money, I could be happy.

If I had better genes, I could lose weight.

If I had more time, I could exercise more.

If I liked vegetables, I could eat healthier.

If I had gone to college, I could be successful.

If this, then that.

But it's the *if* statement that fails. Such utterances are debilitating self-fulfilling prophecies. They hold us back. The best thing to do is remove the *if* clause from your declarations, revealing your true potential:

I could be happy.

I could lose weight.

I could exercise more.

I could eat healthier.

I could be successful.

Because, truth be told...
If you wanted to, you could live a meaningful life.

Please Masturbate in Your Own Room

There exists a warning sign in showers of the dorms at Miami University (Ohio), a college we both attended before not finishing college. The sign says in bold letters, PLEASE MASTURBATE IN YOUR OWN ROOMS. While it's a fairly humorous warning (and likely a student prank), it seems to be a suitable synecdoche for the online world.

Of course it sounds vulgar, but unfortunately the analogy is apt. Many of us get so caught up in displaying ourselves online that we're willing to do just about anything to get attention—*Hey look at me! Look what I'm doing! Pay attention to me!*—as if yelling loud enough will attract and retain quality readers, as if it will attract and retain a large audience, as if it will somehow attract new friends.

When shouting in their empty room doesn't work, people often resort to silly stunts and obscene actions: the drunken Facebook pictures, the banal Twitter updates ("I'm eating a pancake!"), the shirt-off-in-the-mirror photos, the pop-up ads and sleazy marketing, the superfluous cursing in blog posts. All of which is tantamount to public masturbation.

People do these things because it gives them instant

gratification. Someone might "Like" a picture of them inebriated and passed out on the arm of a couch. Someone might retweet their silly tweets. Someone might comment on their obnoxious blog post. That modicum of attention, albeit *negative* attention, can become addictive. And so they feel compelled to do more of the same, upping their gratuitousness threshold each time.

The problem is that this doesn't work—not in the long-term anyway. It never does. Sure, yelling loud enough will attract scads of newcomers—we can't help but slow down and look at the wreckage, but we never stick around to admire the post-accident clean-up. Similarly, someone's public indecency might draw some initial attention, but they'll be left feeling empty and alone when people leave the scene of the accident and never return.

Like masturbating, some activities are private activities, and they aren't meant for public display, be it online or in the physical world. This is one of the reasons the two of us don't write about our personal, intimate relationships online. That stuff is private. Moreover, it wouldn't serve the greater good. And since our focus here is to contribute to people—to show people how they can live more meaningfully—we needn't tell every personal detail of our stories.

Thus, we show you our personal lives—up close and very personal at times—but we make an attempt to leave out the stuff that does not add value to your lives (viz. the stuff that doesn't serve the greater good). Which means we show you the applicable parts, the humorous parts, and the aspects that have changed our lives, in hopes that those same things can change yours. We want to make a difference in the lives of our readers—to engage them in thoughtful conversation—that is why we write here, not to show our private parts.

30 More Life Lessons from 30 Years
By Ryan Nicodemus

Yesterday was my 30th birthday. The big three-oh. To celebrate, here's another 30 life lessons to accompany Joshua's previously published "30 Life Lessons from 30 Years" and our friend Leo Babauta's "38 Life Lessons I've Learned in 38 Years." Oh, and please, whatever you do, don't get me any birthday gifts. Your support is more than enough.

1. It's not about how people feel about you, but how you make them feel. From grade school through my freshman year in high school, I was chubby, crooked-toothed, and had low self-esteem. I was very concerned with how I looked and even more concerned with how people saw me. Unfortunately, looks were everything to me. Plus, I was constantly worried about hanging out with the cool kids. In fact, looking back on my friend choices, I remember blowing off some great people because they weren't who I considered to be "cool." Growing older has shown me that the cool kids aren't always the happy kids. After realizing this, I realized that what people think about you isn't nearly as important as how you make them feel.

2. Consider all advice. "Oh if I knew then what I know now." I couldn't tell you how many times I heard that from my parents and grandparents growing up. Now at age 30, I completely understand what they meant. It's amazing how much smarter our parents appear as we get older. In many instances, if I listened to my parents' and grandparents's advice, I could have avoided learning lessons the hard way. When I realized this, I told myself that even if I didn't agree with what someone was telling me, I would at least consider the advice they gave. This has worked well for me, helping me to look in the mirror and consider if there was something I needed to change.

3. Happiness comes from within. Letting my possessions define who I was quickly lead to an empty feeling inside. Happiness comes from within, not from the things we own.

4. You'll never be happy with more until you're happy with what you have currently. It's as simple as that. In most cases I have discovered that I usually don't get rewarded in life with more until I appreciate the current life I have.

5. Forgiveness is important. I used to do a good job holding grudges and keeping count of who wronged me. There is a profound saying in the Bible: "freely forgive others as you forgive yourself." When I learned how to let things go and easily forgive others, I was a much happier person. In fact, I found the bigger the wrong I forgave, the better I felt.

6. You can count your closest friends on one hand. This is also something I remember my parents and grandparents saying while I was growing up. They were right. As you grow older you find out who is actually your friend and who isn't.

7. Being honest is always the right thing. This is something I learned on accident when admitting to my grandmother that I snuck into her liquor cabinet when I was 18. At the time I was living with her. She told me that if I lied to her when she asked me if it was true or not, she was going to ask me to leave her house because she wouldn't be able to trust me. Even when I've royally screwed up in life, I have found that honesty punishes me less and gains the trust of many.

8. If you lie, you will get caught. This is very true for my life. Plus, if you lie, you will probably have to tell more lies to cover up the original lie. It's a vicious cycle.

9. Although honesty is incredibly important, I don't have to be completely transparent. I've always had this tendency to wear my heart on my sleeve and be very blunt with my comments. I've learned that just because something is true, I don't have to say it—I needn't spew forth every thought that enters my head.

10. People are inherently good. I have been lied to, picked on, and treated badly many times, which has caused me to be a bit cynical and expect the worst out of people. This year I finally realized that even the people who've treated me poorly are still good at some level. None of us is perfect. This has helped me be less cynical.

11. Slow Down. This is something I continue to work on improving. We all need to slow down, breathe, and pace ourselves when we get overwhelmed.

12. Friendly people at work aren't necessarily your friends. This is another lesson learned the hard way. Be careful who you open up to at work.

13. Stay true to yourself. If it doesn't feel right, if it doesn't feel good, if it doesn't feel like *you*, then don't do it. I'm much happier when I follow this advice.

14. Every decision matters. This is something I attempt to instill in my brothers and sisters still in high school. Every decision we make will affect our future. There is no such thing as a zero-sum decision.

15. There is no such thing as a free lunch. Every decision we make costs us something, be it time, emotion, money, etc.

16. "Act as if…" This is a line from the movie *Boiler Room*. It has stuck with me ever since I watched that movie over a decade ago. This could also be interpreted as "be the change in the world you want to see." Either way, this line has helped me throughout my life.

17. "No one can make you feel inferior without your consent." —Eleanor Roosevelt. You needn't care what people think or say about you. What they say or think is only true if you believe it's true. Don't let anyone get the best of you.

18. Some of life's most profound advice is found in the most overused platitudes. "You can be anything you want to be"; "Life's too short"; "Time heals all wounds"; "Good things come to those that wait"; etc. Don't dismiss it just because it's a platitude. It became a platitude for a reason.

19. Don't sweat the small stuff. This is something I have really appreciated with getting older. It's harder for me to get jealous, it's easier for me to forgive, and it's easier for me to overlook the negative things in life.

20. It's all small stuff. Until you have a few life-changing experiences, this isn't as clear. I have had a few close calls with myself, friends, and family, which have shown me how small my problems are.

21. If you don't take care of your health, it will fade fast. I don't think I need to articulate this one any more. If you're over 30, you likely know exactly what I'm talking about.

22. Relationships are important. This lesson brings up all kinds of clichéd thoughts. First, it's all about who you know —who you know can get you far. Second, relationships require work—this is especially true in my relationships with past girlfriends. Knowing this has helped me tremendously by giving me more patience. Third, don't burn a bridge with another person if you can avoid it. You never know who will be deciding your fate.

23. Live life with passion. If I didn't have passion in my life, I would be bored to death. If you're bored, focus on your passions. If you don't have time for your passions, make time.

24. If you're not growing, you're dying. If you're not growing in life, you are simply living out your days.

25. Contribute. Contributing to someone else, or to a community, will make you feel good. Contribution is what makes me feel the most alive. Contributing to others is what keeps me going, it's what gets me up in the mornings, and it's what continues to inspire me.

26. In twenty years you will regret the things you didn't do more than the things you did do. This is something I continually remind myself. For example, when it comes to my bachelor's degree: When I was 25 and without a degree, I asked myself if I wanted to have my degree by the time I was 30, or did I want to be 30 wishing I had my degree. I don't necessarily need it right now, but I'm glad I started on it when I was 25 and not 30.

27. Life is happening now! I let this slip. When I came home from work I forgot. When I stayed up late working for my bosses, I forgot. When I commuted two hours to work, I forgot. Don't forget to live life in the moment.

28. Learn to let go. This was a hard lesson for me, but it serves true. Sometimes it's just better to let things go. I could go on and on about how my employer wronged me, or how that guy cut me off, or how I wanted to be a CEO in 10 years, but in reality none of this matters.

29. Everything changes. Things don't look different day to day, but when you look back 10 years it's all different. There is one thing that's for sure: change is a definite and we should plan accordingly. Don't fool yourself.

30. Procrastination is useless. Don't let your crastination turn pro. No matter how long I put something off, it's still there the next day.

Your Own Advice Is the Hardest Pill to Swallow

Giving advice is pretty easy, isn't it? Anyone can give advice. Anyone can make recommendations. Anyone can tell you what to do. But just because someone gives you advice, that doesn't mean it's the correct advice for you.

And sometimes it's easy to take advice from other people when they are dishing it out. Having relationship trouble? We typically ask a friend for advice. Having a conflict with a co-worker? We ask another co-worker for advice. Having money problems? Well, you get the idea.

But sometimes, all we have to do is look in the mirror and ask ourselves for advice. After all, who knows you better than you? Nobody is more acutely aware of your situation. Nobody is more familiar with every particular scenario and potential outcome than you.

So why do we turn to another person so often for advice? Because it's easy. If someone tells us what to do, we don't even have to think. Coincidentally (or not-so-coincidentally) this is also how fascism works (i.e., someone else makes the decisions for you).

Or sometimes we ask other people for advice to

reaffirm our own advice. But other people rarely have a stake in the outcome of taking their advice, which makes it less valid than your own point of view.

Sure, it's OK to ask others for advice—sometimes it's great to have a clean pair of eyes—but remember, at the end of the day, it is you who has to live with your own decisions.

Mistakes vs. Bad Decisions

"You're only as good as your last mistake / You're only as right as the wrong you make."
—Augustana, "Last Mistake"

A politician cheats on his wife, gets caught, and says he "made a big mistake." A businesswoman omits some revenue on her taxes and says something similar to the IRS. A son lies to his mother and later fesses up to his "mistake." In truth, these examples aren't mistakes—they're bad decisions.

Selecting the wrong answer on a test is a mistake; not studying for that test is a bad decision. The mistake was something you did without intention, while the bad decision was made intentionally, often without regard for the consequence.

It's easy to dismiss your bad decisions by reclassifying them as mistakes. It takes the edge off, softens the blow. But it's much worse than that: reclassifying a bad decision as a mistake removes your sense of responsibility, making it no longer your fault. And it's a lot easier to live with your bad decisions if they aren't your fault. Consequently, you're more likely to make the same bad decision over and over and over again if you simply consider it a mistake.

We all make mistakes. We all make bad decisions. They are part of the human experience. We can celebrate our mistakes—failure is often the key to success. And we can learn from our bad decisions. But let's not confuse one with the other.

You Are Inadequate

You are inadequate. At least that's what advertisers would like you to believe.

You bear witness to proof of your inadequacy every day: you see it on your TV, hear it on your radio, stare back at it on your computer screen and on highway billboards. There are plenty of messages all around you to reinforce your utter inadequacy.

If you're a male, you're not a real man unless you drink this brand of beer and eat this particular cut of meat and drive that brand of sport utility vehicle. If you're a female, you're not a real woman unless you squeeze into that size dress and don this shiny piece of jewelry and tote the purse with all those ostentatious C's or LV's on its leather exterior. Then and only then will you feel adequate—or so they'd have you believe.

But when you obtain these things, what happens? Do you feel long-term adequacy? Nope. Of course not. Your thirst for over-indulgent consumption isn't quenched when you obtain more material possessions. In fact, it's just the opposite: your desire to consume increases—you've set the bar higher and thus the threshold for future satisfaction is higher, too. It's a vicious, never-ending cycle.

You see, consumption is an unquenchable thirst. This is because we create that thirst, we manufactured the desire to consume more. Sure, advertisers play their role, they help us activate the desire we've created, but ultimately the desire is ours to control. Once we realize we have control, we can break the cycle, we can avoid the continuous downward spiral.

There is one way out of consumption's never-ending downward spiral: We must realize that we're already more than adequate without buying more stuff—we are already imperfectly perfect. We must realize that the things we purchase do not define who we are—unless we allow them to.

If we're defined by our things, we'll never be happy. But if we're defined by our actions, we'll have the opportunity to feel fulfilled by our everyday growth, we'll have the opportunity to feel satisfied with our everyday contribution to others, we'll have the opportunity to be content every single day of our lives.

You see, the stuff doesn't make you happy—*you* make you happy.

Decluttering Your Mental Clutter

By Ryan Nicodemus

Those voices inside your head won't be quiet. All you can hear is your boss telling you to have those reports done by Friday or your daughter reminding you that there's soccer practice this Saturday or a parent's voice telling you that they're going to need you to help them drop off their car at the mechanic's.

Most of us have somewhere to be each day, not to mention the everyday fire drills we get put through at work or at home. It can feel very overwhelming, and our minds can get noisy. Some of us even have echoes of voices from experiences of many years ago.

How do you deal with all that internal mental clutter?

Mental clutter is something I've worked on my entire life. I used to feel like, no matter what, I constantly had some sort of mental clutter—I always had something going on in my mind. If it wasn't something new causing that anxious, cluttered feeling, it was something from the past creeping into the present to haunt me. Some days were worse than others, but it was there every day.

And then, after repairing several other areas of my life, I was able to cut down on the mental clutter...

Physical Health

Your mind and your body aren't standing in separate corners of the room. The brain is a delicate organ and we have to treat it right. It's much easier for a physically unhealthy person to experience a poor mental state. If you are interested in learning more, I recommend reading *Change Your Brain Change Your Life* by Daniel G. Amen. I was impressed with this book's in-depth explanation of the ties between the human brain and the human body.

For me, I notice I feel more anxiety when I have an empty stomach, have not exercised in over a week, eat junk food, and don't get enough sleep. I discovered once I changed these things—once I focused on my body through diet and exercise and proper sleep—the mental clutter also began clearing away.

Improving my health was an important first step.

Circumstances

If you're like me—the old me—then you're saying to yourself that you can't change your circumstances. And with that attitude, I was absolutely right.

But once I decided I'd had enough of the mental clutter, I had no choice but to to change my circumstances—I had no choice but to remove myself from circumstances that added to my mental clutter.

I stopped associating with certain people, I changed my spending habits, I downsized my possessions. I started with myself, and I changed my circumstances.

Over time, things change, and instead of letting them change on their own, I decided to change those things myself. Some of those changes were difficult, but the world didn't stop spinning.

I stopped associating with a few folks who encouraged bad habits and the world didn't end.

I was laid-off in September 2011 and I didn't die.

I changed expectations with family on what things I did and didn't want in my life and they supported me.

My circumstances are completely different now from a few months ago and I'm miles happier. Don't take this the wrong way. I'm not saying everyone needs to quit their job, or take any egregious actions, but please understand that your problems likely aren't as bad as you think they are.

Don't be fooled by anyone. You are in control of your circumstances. You are in control of you.

Past Troubles

This was one of my biggest issues: my haunting past. I've made mistakes. Big mistakes. I've let people down, and I've made some plain old dumb decisions. But I've also been extremely hard on myself, unnecessarily hard on myself, neurotic about the mistakes and bad decisions I'd made. Sometimes I'd fall asleep replaying my whole day in my head, every word and conversation looking for mistakes or ways to improve who I was.

Now, every time I feel anxiety caused from some past experience, I ask myself a few different questions: Is that situation relevant now? Was that situation even that serious? Am I blowing it out of proportion? Was that situation in my control? Does what that person said actually have any validity or are they just acting out of fear or anger?

To stop being so hard on myself, I had to learn how to discern the things that mattered and didn't matter, and the above questions helped. I also had to learn what things were in and out of my control. If something was out of my control, I had to accept this fact so I could focus on the things I could control—the things I could change.

What Makes You Tick?

To find out what made me tick, I sat down and drew a vertical line down a piece of paper. I labeled one side "Good Days" and the other side "Bad Days." For each scenario, "Good Day" or "Bad Day," I thought of the foods I ate, people I saw, places I visited etc. I couldn't remember every detail but it gave me a few places to start with when it came to my diet and relationships.

Then, I bought a few tools that helped me with my frame of mind. We all need the right tools to help get rid of the mental clutter. The book I mentioned written by Daniel G. Amen was a great place to start. The book Joshua and I wrote, *Minimalism: Live a Meaningful Life*, show's how we replaced bad habits with good ones when it comes to diet and relationships specifically. I even invested money in a counselor for a few sessions to help me get an unbiased opinion on a few things. To get better, I knew I needed to have the right tools. Those tools can be different for everyone, but don't expect to fix everything on your own.

Quitting Your Job Is Easy

Scores of people ask us how to quit their jobs. Much of the time it feels like they're simply asking for our permission.

The truth is you don't need our permission. Quitting your job is incredibly easy. Simply walk into your boss's office and say, *Screw you, I quit!*

See, that was easy. What happens *after* you quit is the hard part.

First, the simple questions surface: What will I do to make money? How am I going to pay my bills? How will I afford medical coverage? What if I fail? What do I do about the people who depend on me?

Eventually, the more difficult questions begin to peek their ugly little heads into the picture: How will I spend my newfound free time? How will I live a more meaningful life? How will I cope with this new sense of utter aloneness. What if this doesn't work long-term? What will I tell people I "do" if I no longer have a title to give them. Will I die alone?

The most important questions, however, should be asked before you consider leaving your job: Am I living a lie? Why do I want to quit my job? What am I passionate about? What is my mission in life? Should I look for employment that is more in line with my passions and my mission? What would my ideal employer look like? Should I start my own business? Will the Cincinnati Bengals ever make it to the Super Bowl?

With the exception of that last question, these are better, more meaningful questions that get you to the root of why you want to quit your job in the first place: you are unhappy with your current circumstances.

I Will Always Be OK
By Ryan Nicodemus

I will always be OK. *I will* always be successful. *I will* always be happy.

I will. Think about these two words for a moment. Life's revelations are found in the simplest of words. That's why most people will miss the message here. That's why some people who read this will brush it off as babble, as cliché, as a trite platitude.

On the other hand, if you can grasp these words and understand what I'm trying to convey, *you will* have the upper hand in life. And let's be honest, we all want control of our own lives.

The Pressure We Put on Ourselves

People are more stressed than ever. We have more pressure put on us than at any other time in history.

You see it on your TV, the toothpick models and rugged "sexiest men alive" occupying the screen. *This* is what you're *supposed* to look like.

You hear it on your radio, the solipsistic over-indulgence of Hummer-driving rap stars and champagne-guzzling pop stars promulgating irresponsible living. *This* is how you're *supposed* to consume.

You notice it at work, the co-worker gossip about *him* and *her* and, god forbid, *you*. This is how you're supposed to behave. To have the tallest building in town, you must tear down everyone else's.

Suffice it to say, the pressure is all around us.

Or is it?

The truth is that nearly all the pressure we feel is completely internal. Sure, this pressure is influenced by external factors, but that doesn't mean we have to take the bait. We needn't succumb to these influences.

You see, the pressure is only there if you allow it to be. Sure, everyone will judge you, but no one actually cares about the details of your life. No one cares if you fit into that size 0 dress or if you drive a fancy sports car or if you have the tallest building in town. Once you realize this, you can give yourself permission to get rid of the pressure. You are already perfect without it.

You Are Not Impressing Me

Our *Please-Like-Me* Culture has transformed into something hideous. We've been enveloped by an epidemic of pointless, attention-grabbing solipsism. Look around, the world is attempting to impress you.

Truth be told, we needn't impress anyone, and yet we all try. Relentlessly we try, doing the strangest things to get the attention and, ultimately, the approval of others.

Oh, you purchased a brand new Lexus? You're a published author? Your job title is X and you earn six-figures?

So what!

Take it from two guys who had it all. We had to get "everything we ever wanted" to realize that everything we ever wanted wasn't what we wanted at all. It was empty, meaningless, depressing.

Your material possessions, your social status, and even your so-called accomplishments don't impress anyone. They certainly don't impress us. YOU impress us. Not the things around you. We are impressed by your commitment to change, by your ability to grow, by your desire to contribute beyond yourself. Everything else is just a social construct, devoid of meaning.

There's nothing inherently wrong with owning

possessions or accomplishing goals or earning money. Just don't think those things impress anyone. They don't. At least not in a meaningful way.

In Too Deep

"Don't let me slip over the railing, eyes wide and arms are flailing / Don't let me slip, don't let me slip into the deep end."
—Slow Runner, "Deep End"

It's easy to believe that the earth turns slowly. It's always there; we're a part of it, deep in the middle of its rotation.

In many ways, consumerism is no different. It's all around us, everywhere we turn, seemingly unstoppable—hell's own self-consuming heart.

But the earth doesn't turn slowly; it's spinning at over a thousand miles an hour.

This became easy for us to understand once we stepped back and paid attention, once we became aware of our surroundings.

Similarly, we needn't look around at all this mass-consumption and over-indulgence and believe it's normal.

It's not.

Things haven't always been this way, this chaotic, this meaningless. And the future needn't be either.

A sunrise is on the horizon, and we can see it once we

open our eyes, become more aware of what's important, and realize we're in too deep.

Letting Go of Control

It's easy to pretend we're in control of every aspect of our lives. Societal norms and tireless advertisements reinforce this message: *you* run the show; life is what *you* make of it; have it *your* way. *You* are the sovereign king of your own bite-sized kingdom.

But much of what occurs around us day-to-day is utterly outside our jurisdiction. We don't know if that oncoming Ford pick-up is going to veer left-of-center and collide head-on with our vehicle. We can't possibly predict that a maniac is going to rob the bank as we drop-in during our lunch break to cash a paycheck. We can't anticipate the brutal storm that floods every basement in the neighborhood.

No matter the amount of rigorous planning, the unexpected will occur.

For example: during summer 2012, we announced Ryan's private mentoring sessions on our website, and the first-day response was astounding. Everything was progressing swimmingly—Ryan's mentoring calendar filled up for nearly two months—but then, unexpectedly, our website crashed, our files were corrupted, and it would take a couple days to restore everything. In the meantime, no one could access our site, and thus no one else would know about Ryan's big announcement. Upwards of 5,000 people visit our site each day, so being out of commission for two days was far from ideal. Rome was burning and we couldn't locate an extinguisher. The problem was simply outside our control.

We'd never experienced a major website outage before, and we didn't know what to do. As far as we could see, we had two clear options: 1) panic, or 2) let our hosting company work on the problem. If we panicked, the site would still be down, but at least we'd be in control, right? Panicking, after all, is just a strange way to regain order in an otherwise disorderly situation. This type of control, however, does no good, and is in fact harmful, unproductive, and detrimental to our mental health. However, if we relied on our hosting company to fix the problem, then we were letting go of control, placing our faith in someone else to do the right thing, which can feel like being stripped naked, exposed while waiting for someone to fetch us dry clothes.

The simple fact is that we are not in control. Not of everything, at least. Instead, we control our odds, and if we place ourselves in the most ideal situations often enough, then, odds are, things will sway our way more often than not. Everything else requires a little leap of faith.

Perhaps letting go of control is the best way to regain total control.

Everything Can Change in a Year

The Difference a Year Can Make

We started *The Minimalists* one year ago (a year before writing this). Since then almost everything in our lives has changed.

A year ago we both worked for large corporations. Now we work for ourselves and pursue our passions every day.

A year ago we were unhappy with our lives. Now we're fulfilled and satisfied with our lives.

A year ago we could hardly spell HTML, let alone build a website. Now we have our website, *The Minimalists*, as well as Joshua's fiction site.

A year ago we had zero people reading our words (other than some vapid corporate emails). Now we have over 100,000 monthly readers, and our essays have been read by over half-a-million people in 151 countries this year.

A year ago zero people subscribed to our site. Now over 10,000 people subscribe via email.

A year ago no one was interested in following us on Twitter or Facebook. Now more than 15,000 people interact with us via those mediums.

A year ago we were really inspired by Leo Babauta,

Colin Wright, Joshua Becker, Julien Smith, and other writers like them. And we still are inspired by them. A year later we've met these guys, been featured on their amazing websites, and established great relationships with them and dozens of similar people who have helped shaped our lives in meaningful ways.

A year ago we hadn't published anything. Now we've published three books: an essay collection, Joshua's short story collection, and our first full-length nonfiction book.

A year ago we had spreadsheets full of goals, and we would beat ourselves up when we didn't achieve those goals. Now Ryan lives with one goal at a time, and Joshua has no goals at all.

A year ago we strived to make everything perfect. Now we embrace the imperfection of our daily lives.

A year ago we were a couple of guys stuck in Dayton, Ohio. Now we're traveling the country on a 33-city meetup tour and meeting the most amazing people we've ever met, giving thousands of free hugs to anyone who wants one.

A year ago there was a considerable amount of discontent in our lives. Now we're happy, and when we look in life's rearview mirror, everything is different.

A Reason for These Stats

We aren't trying to impress you with our "accomplishments." Rather, we want to impress upon you the power of a year. As human beings, we often overestimate what we can accomplish in a short period of time (e.g., six-pack abs in two weeks), but we drastically underestimate what we can accomplish in a year or two.

Most of the above mentioned "accomplishments" weren't goals we developed at the beginning of the year. They just happened, organically, as we worked hard to add value to other people's lives. Thus, we discovered that when we add value to other people's lives, everything else tends to fall into place.

The big life changes don't happen overnight. Give yourself some time. Put in a lot of effort and keep at it. You'll be surprised with what can happen in a year.

PART FOUR

PERSONAL RELATIONSHIPS

Asking Friends & Family to Embrace Change

Change isn't easy. More often than not, we don't change because we get in our own way. Other times we don't make a change because we're afraid of what people will think about us, afraid of what they will say about us, afraid they will treat us differently. Ultimately, we are afraid of rejection.

When we approached minimalism, we realized that many of our closest friends and family members were supportive of the changes we wanted to make. And in other cases, many of them were neutral bystanders, ambivalent to the simplification going on around us.

But in some instances, some of the people closest to us didn't approve of our new paths, mistaking our journey for a direct attack on *their* way of life, as if by questioning our own lives we were also questioning their lifestyles by proxy. Clearly this was not our intent. Our journey involved questioning our own lives, not theirs. We were simply looking for happiness, using minimalism as a tool to search for deeper meaning in our lives.

And yet some people thought the changes we were making were silly, stupid, and even crazy (literally). After all, we had worked hard for more than a decade to accumulate all these fancy material possessions and important job titles and the American Dream, all of which were supposed to make us happy, right?

And so when the consumerist, over-indulgent lives we were leading didn't make us happy, there had to be something wrong with *us*. At least that's what the naysayers said: Maybe Joshua and Ryan went crazy. Maybe they are experiencing a *mid*-midlife crisis. Maybe they joined a cult (someone legitimately accused us of joining a cult, likening minimalism to Jonestown and Branch Davidian).

We had to explain a few things to these naysayers:

It's not you, it's me. We've all heard this line before. It's been parodied a thousand times. But there is a profound truth to be discovered here. We weren't questioning anyone else's lifestyle but our own. Many people weren't happy with their own situations, and they aspired to be like us because we had the lifestyle they wanted to emulate: we had the material possessions, we had the salaries, we had the awards, we had the ostensible power, we were on the fast-track to corporate success. But we looked around us and realized that most of the people above us, people several rungs higher on the corporate ladder, weren't happy either. In fact, they were far less happy than we were—and we weren't happy at all. What were we supposed to do—keep working incredibly hard and aspire to continue to be unhappy? It's alright to tell naysayers that you're making changes in your life so you can be happy. Better yet, you can do what we did and ask those naysayers a question: "You want me to be happy, don't you?"

Circumstances change. If our 28 year-old selves could have time-traveled back to 1999 to tell our 18-year-old selves about everything we were going to "accomplish" over the next decade, the teenage Joshua and Ryan would have been elated. *You mean I'm going to have this, that, and this? You mean I'll be able to afford this?* But the happiness would have soon faded, and by 28 (or perhaps much sooner) a cloak of discontent would have enveloped our lives. That's because circumstances change. And thus *we* must change; we must continue to evolve and grow if we expect to be happy. What adds value to your life today may not add value to your life tomorrow.

You too can change. Minimalism may not be the answer for you. But if you're not happy, you too can build your change muscle and, over time, change your circumstances. There are many paths to happiness. Minimalism simply allowed us to clear the preverbal clutter from our own paths so we could find that happiness sooner.

Show people the benefits. As we journeyed farther down our paths, many of the naysayers jumped on board. Not because we asked them too—we've never asked anyone to embrace minimalism—but because they saw the happiness we'd welcomed into our lives. They saw that for the first time in our adult lives we were truly excited and joyous, and we were content with who we were. They saw that perhaps we *didn't* have it figured out before, and maybe we didn't know all the answers now, but we certainly appeared to be on the right track. The actions alone didn't convince them, but once they saw the benefits, they better understood the changes we'd undergone.

Goodbye. There were, however, some relationships we had to get rid of. It wasn't easy, but certain people—friends and family—weren't adding value to our lives; they were sources of negativity, and they prevented us from growing. We treated this option as a last resort, but it's important to know that, as we grow, even our relationships can change. Today, many of our old friends are still our friends—while others are not—but we've also established new, empowering relationships that encourage our constant growth and help us enjoy what we contribute to the relationship.

Vying for Attention

It's hard to realize that we are not the all-hours center of the attention.

We all have the same 24 hours in a day, and yet we often neglect other people's time while holding ours on a pedestal. Our own time is precious to us, and yet we're constantly vying for other people's attention, acting as if their attention isn't just as precious as ours.

When we're attempting to grab someone's attention, we should do our part:

1. Be succinct. Brevity is indeed the soul of wit. Or, perhaps, *brevity is wit*. Thus, we needn't wedge in unnecessary information or details. It's possible to use minimalism to converse with others. Don't leave out important information —don't be vague—but find a balance; it's lurking there beneath the clutter of unnecessary details.

2. Have a point. Why do you want this person's attention? To entertain her? To inform her? To ask her a question? Be as specific as you can.

3. Add value. This is the most important part. If you are not adding value, then you're just taking someone's valuable time. Ask yourself: *Does this add value?*

Seven Steps to Meaningful Conversations

Our relationships are one of the most important aspects of living a meaningful life. Conversing with a close friend can be an experience filled with meaning. And yet we often don't value these conversations like we should, we don't pay enough attention to the important people around us.

Just like we use minimalism to get rid of excess stuff in favor of essential things, we can use it to rid ourselves of superfluous conversation in favor of essential, meaningful conversations.

Seven Ways to Make Conversations Meaningful

1. Make your words count. There is no need to count your words, just make sure they count. You can make sure your words add value to your conversations. It is important to be acutely aware of *what* you are saying and, more important, *why* you are saying it.

2. Expand your vocabulary. An extensive vocabulary allows you to be more precise, and precision allows you to better convey what you mean in a short span.

3. Be succinct. Brevity is vigor.

4. Avoid unnecessary conversations. Our words become sloppy when we are forced to partake in a multitude of unnecessary conversations each day. Many of these conversations can be avoided or radically attenuated. Can you think of more than one conversation you could have avoided or shortened yesterday? What could you have done to avoid that conversation?

5. Converse more with loved ones. The people who really matter in your life—your friends, family, and loved ones—deserve quality conversation from you. By ridding yourself of the aforementioned unnecessary conversations, you can allocate more time to converse with loved ones and establish deeper connections.

6. Listen more than you talk. It sounds cliché to say this, but some of the most profound truths are found in clichés. This happens to be one of those profound truths. Listening —honest, attentive listening—is not easy, and it doesn't come naturally to most. Thus, we must make an effort to listen when we are engaged in conversation.

7. Ask and listen. An easy way to be an engaged listener is to ask and then listen. This allows you to actively participate in the listening process by asking interesting questions and allowing the other person to respond uninterrupted. (N.B. the quality of your questions is paramount here.)

Do You Know What Your Neighbors Are Up To?

By Ryan Nicodemus

Do you know your neighbors? I mean do you really *know* your neighbors?

I live in a condo development in which there are roughly 80 units, and until recently I didn't know any of the people living there other than a few of their names and faces. I didn't value the relationships, or potential relationships, until recently.

When I first moved into this neighborhood I looked at the situation like any other bachelor who saw an opportunity to live in a nice place that was virtually maintenance free. With a busy life I enjoyed the thought of not spending hours on upkeep every week, doing odds and ends that people who own a house find themselves doing regularly.

Or so I thought…

After the first few months of living there I realized there was a plethora of issues within the condo association. They hardly did anything around the place besides haphazardly mow the grass and keep up on small odds and ends (e.g., roof leaks, siding repairs, etc.). With the tough economic times they had not been able to add much value to the property.

At one point I was solicited by several board members to impeach other members on the board. I was asked to pick sides and support the election of a new board. Since I didn't know any of my neighbors it was hard to choose which side was right, and it was difficult to decipher who was right and who was wrong—it felt like everyone was being negative (including myself).

Because of the negativity permeating the condo, I wanted to leave after only a year of living there. And after adopting a minimalist lifestyle I especially wanted out of there, realizing I had this gigantic place all to myself. It was incredibly overwhelming.

The easiest answer I could come up with to fix this problem was to ignore the issues around the condo association and put my condo up for sale, which I did, but I was unable to find a buyer. I spent many days frustrated and blamed the board for the bickering and inability to manage the budget. This was *their fault*, not mine. I fell into this *Why me?* stage, which only exacerbated my frustration.

Recently I had a neighbor (who was on the board) send out an email asking for everyone in the community to pitch in and volunteer to do some upkeep around the community—to make the place a little nicer and increase morale. My first thought when I saw this email was "why do I pay condo dues if I have to do the upkeep myself?" Then I realized that this attitude towards the board, and the *Why me?* attitude, was only worsening the situation. I wasn't helping the problem; I was part of the problem. So I did the exact opposite of what I wanted to do: I replied and said, yes I would help.

When the workday rolled around there were six owners including myself (out of roughly 80) who showed up to help. I didn't let this discourage me, because, again, I was sick of fueling my frustration. I worked my tail off and did what needed to be done for the day.

As we worked, I got to know my five neighbors and realized they were just as frustrated as me. I also developed a good relationship with the board member who arranged the community workday. I felt better about the changes he was trying to make. It had taken the board more than five years to sink the association, and after talking with him I realized it was going to take a couple years to repair the damage.

Until I actually got to know my neighbors that day I honestly thought everyone was out for themselves (which may still be the case with some of them), but they were just like me. After we all spent the day with each other, we felt much closer, a closeness that formed a bond that's beneficial to our entire community.

Getting Laid Off from My Job Is One of the Best Things that Ever Happened to Me

By Ryan Nicodemus

A Day to Remember

I sat down in the harshly lit conference room and slid his birthday present across the table. It was September 29, 2011—my boss's birthday. And it was less than a month before *my* 30th birthday. It was also the day I lost my job.

My boss, my boss's boss, and a woman from human resources were sitting on the other side of the large, meticulously-polished conference table. My boss shook his head and a frown materialized on his face. I knew it wasn't good news—sitting in a room with your boss, his boss, and HR typically isn't a recipe for good news—but my first thought was, "It really sucks for him that he has to let me go on his birthday."

"We've eliminated your position with the latest round of cuts. This change is effective immediately," one of them said. Seven months after Joshua left his job, I was laid off with no notice, with no friendly warning, with no heads-up —just blind-sided after working unimaginably hard for a corporation. Seven years and eight job titles later, living the "corporate dream" was over in an instant.

"Do you have any additional questions before HR goes over the details with you?"

Nudged Into a More Meaningful Life

No, I didn't have any additional questions. I just sat there and thought, "This is the best thing that could have happened to me."

Suddenly, a gigantic weight had been lifted off my shoulders. I've never been the kind of person who mopes around and feels sorry for himself. I knew it was time for me to move on, and this was the nudge I needed to jump off Corporate America's cliff … ahem, I mean *ladder*.

It was the nudge I needed to focus full-time on my passions, the nudge I needed to focus my time on the important things in life—my health, my relationships, my growth as an individual, and contributing to other people in meaningful ways. This was the drastic change I needed.

Thankfully, my gradual transition into minimalism in 2010 and 2011 allowed me to buy less stuff, spend less money, cut most of my bills, payoff most of my debt, save a little money, and live a more meaningful life with less stuff. I'll still need to make other cutbacks: I contacted a new realtor to sell my condo, I'm selling my car, etc. But none of that matters. Only one thing matters right now: I'm free!

Pursuing My Passions and Contributing More

Adding value to other people's lives has been my passion for as long as I can remember. Adding value was the thing I enjoyed most about my corporate career—I led and managed a large team of people, and I enjoyed coaching and mentoring those people more than anything else at that job. Unfortunately, a lot of things occurred in the corporate world that prevented me from allocating all my time to *adding value* to those people.

Thanks to the success of our website and our books, I'll be able to do what I love—I'll be able to contribute to other people—and not worry about finding another corporate job.

Moreover, I haven't had as much time as I've wanted to respond to comments, return emails, or have conversations with readers. Now I'll get to spend more time with all of you. I'll get to put more time into providing quality content and authentic advice based on my experiences.

My Relationships: My Friends and Family

Maintaining the quality of my relationships has been a struggle for me ever since I started my corporate climb. As I advanced my career and climbed the corporate ladder, I often worked 50-70 hours a week, and I lost track of family and close friends. I started to feel like my job was more important than my relationships. I believed they would understand why I wasn't around as much. Some of them understood, but it didn't feel good. And it certainly didn't feel right. I'm not going to brush off my friends and family anymore.

My Health: Diet and Exercise

Living the corporate life was often a great excuse to let my diet go (*I'll just grab a quick snack before the meeting!*). It was also a great excuse to skip daily exercising (*I'm just too busy to exercise today!*). Those excuses (albeit bullshit excuses) are gone now, and I'm committed to living a healthier life, one in which I'm accountable for and focused on my own diet and exercise.

Now What?

I'm not going to lie, I still have what my friend Leo Babauta refers to as that *joyfear* feeling. Of course there are a few things that I am fearful about—*What if I fail? What if people don't respect me as much? What if , what if, what if?*—but I mostly feel joy.

I plan to live a more purpose-driven life, focused on what's truly important. No, I don't think you need to leave your job to live a meaningful life; but, for me, it was the nudge I needed to get the balance back in my life (working 70 hours a week, perpetually on call, prevented me from finding balance).

For those of you who may be facing a similar situation (i.e., you're uncertain about your job, you're unsure if you should go pursue your passions, etc.), you might be looking for advice. Well, I don't have all the answers. But what I do have is my commitment to add value whenever I can.

The Power of a Hug and Five Other Lessons Learned on the Road

The old apothegm about the teacher learning more than his students is true. Suffice it to say, we learned a lot during our 2012 33-city meetup tour.

Six Lessons Learned on the Road

The 100%. We've learned that the minimalism movement is applicable to everyone, from the Occupy Wall Street folks who showed up in St. Petersburg, to the retired CEO who owned four homes and attended our Atlanta meetup. Irrespective of our income level or social status—whether we're part of the 99% or the 1%—we're all looking for answers. Minimalism can clear the excess from our lives and help us find those answers.

The Growth. We grow whenever we get outside our comfort zones. This isn't easy. Getting outside our comfort zone involves embracing change, facing our fears, killing our doubts, dealing with our internal flinch, and embracing uncertainty. But it is then and only then that you grow as an individual. And when you grow, there is so much more of yourself to give to others.

The Packing Party. So many people have been intrigued and inspired by Ryan's packing party during this tour (including a UK writer who is working the full story into his book). More info on our website: www.theminimalists.com/day3

The Kindness. During our first eleven cities, we had to pay for only one motel. All other nights we stayed with some amazing people who took us in and accepted us as friends.

The Help. Every city has had an amazing meetup leader who was willing to find a venue and coordinate the event. We couldn't have done it without them. When you add value to other people's lives, they are willing to add value to yours. Contribution begets contribution. Contribution is inherently reciprocal.

The Hugs. We've hugged thousands of people in the past few months. People react differently to a hug than a handshake. Try it out. Hug someone you hardly know today. It just might change their life. It just might change yours.

The Number One Lesson of Minimalism

"Everyone that I know / every place that I go / Every story that I'm told / it's love that we're looking for."
—Mat Kearney, "Everyone I Know"

We've learned more than we ever dreamed throughout our journey into minimalism. Likewise during our 33-city meetup tour. And we're still learning. But the most important lesson we've learned is that minimalism appeals to only one group of people:

People with an open mind.

During our coast to coast travels, we experienced a diversity text book of people from every walk of life. Over 1,900 people attended our meetups, from Occupy Wall Street folks to former CEOs, from attorneys to stand-up comics, from 11-year-old boys to 83-year-old great-grandmothers, from every ethnicity to every socioeconomic background, from high school dropouts to college professors, from marathon runners to people struggling to lose weight, from single moms to parents bringing their teenagers to hear us speak.

You are not alone. Minimalism is applicable to anyone. Anyone with an open mind, that is. We're all searching for the same things. We're all searching for more meaningful lives. We're all searching for something to love.

A Supposedly Fun Thing We'll Never Get To Do Again

The last nine months have birthed a new Joshua and Ryan. We have grown immensely since last Thanksgiving (2011) when we decided to embark on a 5-leg, 33-city meetup tour, an irreplicable experience, something we'll likely never get to do again. Suffice it to say, we have learned more—experienced far more—than we expected. Below are some selections from our journals.

Leg 1: November 2011

We have had our car towed in St. Petersburg, Florida. We have now "worked" from the same beach where Joshua scattered his mother's ashes two years prior. We have hugged Occupiers and attorneys and Couch Surfers and retired-CEOs. We have met a Knoxville man who fasted for 40 days.

Leg 2: December 2011

We have been pulled over and searched for drugs by the Kansas state highway patrol. We have slept on a kind couple's floor in Missouri and listened as their Tourettic neighbor howled obscenities throughout the night. We have slept in our car in the middle of the Arizona desert a few feet from poisonous insects and snakes. We have (well, Joshua has) vomited in a bathroom in San Francisco minutes before speaking to our largest crowd of the tour. We have drunk the best tea in the world with our friend Leo. We have, from a distance, mistaken the bright lights of Reno for the bright lights of Vegas. We have been stranded in a blizzard in rural Wyoming. We have searched (unsuccessfully) for John Stockton's bronze statue in Salt Lake City. We have slept in a loft in Milwaukee. We have awkwardly signed autographs in Chicago on New Years Eve-Eve. We have had conversations with an 83-year-old woman and an 11-year-old boy.

Leg 3: March 2012

We have showered with Texas well-water. We have signed more than one Kindle with a silver Sharpie. We have walked in the rain with our friend Chase Night and two beautiful red-headed twins in Little Rock. We have appeared on NPR in St. Louis with the legendary Don Marsh. We have exercised at rest stops in dozens of states. We have been recognized by readers on the streets of Nashville and Dayton and, later, in Seattle. We have thanked people like our friend John Schultz for driving up to 8 hours to meet us in Arkansas and Oklahoma and Kansas.

Leg 4: May 2012

We have eaten fish tacos in Rochester. We have smashed a writing hand—Joshua's right hand—in a faulty window and bled all over Coney Island. We have read a 715-word sentence from Joshua's novella, *Days After the Crash*, aloud in front of a crowd in NYC. We have fallen *up* the stairs while exiting the subway in Manhattan. We have witnessed a white Scottish terrier wearing an argyle sweater smoking a Camel Light in Brooklyn. We have taken our message to the streets of Boston when our venue became too crowded. We have fed homeless people on the streets of Pittsburgh and Cleveland. We have graded homework for Joshua's writing class and taken phone calls for Ryan's private mentoring sessions while on the road. We have given an MLK-style speech at the steps of the Lincoln Memorial. We have seen the largest condom store we've ever seen in Philadelphia.

Leg 5: July 2012

We have driven from Ohio to Des Moines and Portland and Seattle and Vancouver and back. We have shoveled horse poop in front of a polygamist family while the sun set into the Utah mountains. We have visited Mount Rushmore and had much of the experience tainted by myriad advertisements and entire towns predicated on buying shit. We have driven past grass so green that we weren't sure if we were in Iowa or Ireland. We have mistaken much of South Dakota, with its bails of hay atop rolling hills nestled against flat fields, for a giant PC wallpaper image. We have witnessed Independence Day fireworks in downtown Boise. We have parked on the side of the road to take in the ferocious forest fires of Wyoming, bright and blood-orange and uncontrollable as they lit up the night sky. We have spoken alongside our friend Joshua Becker at Chris Guillebeau's *World Domination Summit*. We have slept in a supposedly sleepless Seattle. We have borne witness to what is perhaps the most visually astonishing place on earth: Western Montana, driving past its flannel plains and evergreen mountains and skylines of a cowboy cliché, and past its cobalt rivers overhung with century-old pines and flecklets of sunlight through them on the water bending downriver, to the place beyond its sprawling canyons, where fields divided by train cars simmer in the afternoon heat. We have watched the sun set cinematically over the water during our final meetup in Vancouver. We have spent time in Canada, staying up late and laughing, playing guitar and singing songs, spending quality time with some of the most amazing people we've ever met.

A Panoramic View

We have seen both coasts. We have driven more than 20,000 miles in our tour bus (Toyota Corolla). We have set foot in 40 US states. We have traveled more during our 31st years on earth than the previous 30 combined. We have enjoyed 33 outstanding meetups in 33 unique cities. We have spoken in-front of nearly 2,000 people with audiences ranging from two people to nearly two hundred. We have laughed and cried and laughed at the fact we were crying. We have eaten meals and had meaningful conversations with outstanding people doing outstanding things, all of whom we first met on the Internet. We have made new friends. We have been inspired by scores of people and their amazing stories of transformation. We have, in our own small way, helped spread the message of simple living. We have stopped talking about living and started living.

PART FIVE

AFTER MATER

THE MINIMALISTS, Joshua Fields Millburn and Ryan Nicodemus, write essays about living a meaningful life with less stuff for their online audience of more than 100,000 monthly readers. They have published several bestselling books about simple living and have been featured in the *Wall Street Journal*, CBS, NBC, FOX, NPR, CBC, *Zen Habits*, and numerous other outlets. Find more information at The Minimalists.com.

BOOKS BY THE MINIMALISTS

NONFICTION
Minimalism: Live a Meaningful Life
Everything That Remains

ESSAY COLLECTIONS
A Day in the Life of a Minimalist
Essential Essays
Simplicity

FICTION (by JFM)
Falling While Sitting Down: Stories
Days After the Crash: A Novella
As a Decade Fades: A Novel

ACKNOWLEDGEMENTS

SPECIAL THANKS TO the people who helped make this collection appreciably better with their editing and proofreading efforts: Virginia Allen, Emily High Daniels, Derrick Quandt, Damian Bogel, John Foley, and Wendy Begley. Thank you to our friends Colin Wright and Thom Chambers at Asymmetrical Press and Jeff Sarris, Marla Sarris, and Dave LaTulippe at Spyr Media. And thank you to our gracious readers. We appreciate you. We write these words for you.

CPSIA information can be obtained at www.ICGtesting.com
Printed in the USA
BVOW04s2204050214

344115BV00003B/123/P